A Crabtree Roots Book

DELIVERY PERSON

DOUGLAS BENDER

People
I Meet

CRABTREE
Publishing Company
www.crabtreebooks.com

School-to-Home Support for Caregivers and Teachers

This book helps children grow by letting them practice reading. Here are a few guiding questions to help the reader with building his or her comprehension skills. Possible answers appear here in red.

Before Reading:

• What do I think this book is about?
  - *This book is about delivery people.*
  - *This book is about what a delivery person does at work.*

• What do I want to learn about this topic?
  - *I want to learn what a delivery person looks like.*
  - *I want to learn what a delivery person does.*

During Reading:

• I wonder why...
  - *I wonder why some people become delivery people.*
  - *I wonder why delivery people wear uniforms.*

• What have I learned so far?
  - *I have learned that some delivery people drive trucks.*
  - *I have learned that delivery people help deliver packages.*

After Reading:

• What details did I learn about this topic?
  - *I have learned that delivery people wear uniforms.*
  - *I have learned that delivery people have to be strong to carry a lot of packages.*

• Read the book again and look for the vocabulary words.
  - *I see the word **scanner** on page 6 and the word **uniform** on page 8. The other vocabulary words are found on page 14.*

This is a **delivery person**.

A delivery person delivers **packages**.

A delivery person has a **scanner**.

A delivery person has a **uniform**.

Some delivery people have a **van**.

Do you know a delivery person?

Word List
Sight Words

a	is	you
do	some	
has	this	

Words to Know

delivery person **packages**

scanner **uniform** **van**

34 Words

This is a **delivery person**.

A delivery person delivers **packages**.

A delivery person has a **scanner**.

A delivery person has a **uniform**.

Some delivery people have a **van**.

Do you know a delivery person?

People I Meet
DELIVERY
PERSON

Written by: Douglas Bender
Designed by: Rhea Wallace
Series Development: James Earley
Proofreader: Ellen Rodger
Educational Consultant: Marie Lemke M.Ed.

Photographs:
Shutterstock: AlexS: cover; Monkey Business Images:
p. 1; MichaelJung: p. 3, 14; Drazen Zigic: p. 5, 14; Rido:
p. 7, 14; puhha: p. 9, 13, 14; Gorodenkeff: p. 10, 14

Library and Archives Canada Cataloguing in Publication

Title: Delivery person / Douglas Bender.
Names: Bender, Douglas, 1992- author.
Description: Series statement: People I meet | "A Crabtree
    roots book".
Identifiers: Canadiana (print) 20210178620 |
    Canadiana (ebook) 20210178639 |
    ISBN 9781427141125 (hardcover) |
    ISBN 9781427141187 (softcover) |
    ISBN 9781427133472 (HTML) |
    ISBN 9781427134073 (EPUB) |
    ISBN 9781427141248 (read-along ebook)
Subjects: LCSH: Delivery of goods—Juvenile literature.
Classification: LCC HF5761 .B46 2022 | DDC j658.7/88—dc23

Library of Congress Cataloging-in-Publication Data

CIP available at the Library of Congress

Crabtree Publishing Company

www.crabtreebooks.com   1-800-387-7650

Printed in the U.S.A./062021/CG20210401

Published in the United States
Crabtree Publishing
347 Fifth Avenue, Suite 1402-145
New York, NY, 10016

Published in Canada
Crabtree Publishing
616 Welland Ave.
St. Catharines, Ontario L2M 5V6